Expert Tips To Focus Fast In 3 Days

Skyrocket Your Success & Enjoy More Time With Your Loved Ones & Friends

Patrick Bradley

Text Copyright © Patrick Bradley

All rights reserved. No part of this guide may be reproduced in any form without permission in writing from the publisher except in the case of brief quotations embodied in critical articles or reviews.

Legal & Disclaimer

The information contained in this book and its contents is not designed to replace or take the place of any form of medical or professional advice; and is not meant to replace the need for independent medical, financial, legal or other professional advice or services, as may be required. The content and information in this book have been provided for educational and entertainment purposes only.

The content and information contained in this book have been compiled from sources deemed reliable, and it is accurate to the best of the Author's knowledge, information, and belief. However, the Author cannot guarantee its accuracy and validity and cannot be held liable for any errors and/or omissions. Further, changes are periodically made to this book as and when needed. Where appropriate and/or necessary, you must consult a professional (including but not limited to your doctor, attorney, financial advisor or such other professional advisor) before using any of the suggested remedies, techniques, or information in this book.

Upon using the contents and information contained in this book, you agree to hold harmless the Author from and against any damages, costs, and expenses, including any legal fees potentially resulting from the application of any of the information provided by this book. This disclaimer applies to any loss, damages or injury caused by the use and application, whether directly or indirectly, of any advice or information presented, whether for breach of contract, tort, negligence, personal injury, criminal intent, or under any other cause of action.

You agree to accept all risks of using the information presented inside this book.

You agree that by continuing to read this book, where appropriate and/or necessary, you shall consult a professional (including but not limited to your doctor, attorney, or financial advisor or such other advisor as needed) before using any of the suggested remedies, techniques, or information in this book.

TABLE OF CONTENTS

Chapter 1 3
Challenges People Face in Focusing and How to Overcome Them .. 3

    5 Surprising Challenges in Focusing That Even Professionals & Athletes Face 5

    6 Little Known Foods That Will Make You Lose Your Focus 6

    Success Stories to Prove That You Too Can Overcome Focusing Challenges 8

Chapter 2 11
37 Expert Techniques to Boost & Improve Your Focus and Concentration within 3 Days 11

    Understand the Effects of Poorly Organized Workspace on Your Productivity 17

    How Managing and Organizing Your Emails Boosts Your Focus 17

    How to Optimize Your Concentration and Energy Levels throughout the Day 20

    Music That Gets You into Focus Quickly 21

Chapter 3 23
10-Minutes Daily Expert Practical Tips You Can Implement To Improve Your Focus 23

    Little Known Secrets That Leaders Use To Improve Their Focus 25

    How to Focus Despite Distractions around You 26

    The relationship between Negative Thoughts and Focus and How to Get Rid of Negativity 27

How to Prevent Your Popular Gadgets from Reducing Your Attention Span 29

How to Permanently Get Rid Of Bad Habits That Deteriorate Your Focus 30

Effective Exercise to Improve Productivity and Focus 31

10 Affirmations to Strengthens Your Focusing Abilities 32

Chapter 4 35

Summary of Key Action Plans 35

Conclusion 38

INTRODUCTION

Let's start with some facts; according to research, our attention span has dramatically decreased in 15 years. In 2000, the average attention span of a person was 12 seconds, but it has dropped drastically to about 8.25 seconds now. In fact, this attention span is shorter than that of a goldfish which has an attention span of 9 seconds. Nowadays humans have lost their focusing abilities and this is translating to poor performance and decline in our productivity levels.

We are more distracted than ever before. On average, a worker in an office will check their emails 30 times every hour. People pick up their phones more than 1,500 times a week which takes up about 3 hours and 16 minutes a day.

With so much competition for our attention, it is increasingly difficult to accomplish anything constructive, BUT all is not lost and it is possible to regain your focus and concentration.

Concentration refers to the ability to focus all your attention on a single task or objective. Having single-minded attention is what can help you boost your productivity. This is not something that will come no easily especially nowadays that we are living in a very distracting world. It requires an active mind and willpower to be able to achieve a strong focusing ability.

If you find that your concentration and focusing ability is not that good, you should not despair. Concentration is a soft skill which could be learned and acquired through practice and it can help us make the most out of your day.

Learn what is affecting your concentration and how to deal with the challenges. Learn from the experts and how they manage to stay focused on the things they do. Do you know that it is impossible to regain your concentration and focus in just 3 days? Learn how you can achieve that in this ebook.

We are also going to give you expert tips and practical exercises that you can try under 10 minutes a day to boost your focus and increase your productivity. Do not let the lack of concentration ruin your life; learn how you can achieve success, happiness and maximum productivity using this guide specially prepared for you.

Chapter 1

Challenges People Face in Focusing and How to Overcome Them

Not a single person is perfect in everything; there must be some shortcomings. This is also the case with the focusing ability. Most people struggle to put their mind together and do something constructive. This is even worse in the time we are living in with so many things happening around us.

There is nothing as frustrating as having time to work but later finding out that you have done nothing. However, you should not despair because you are not alone. According to Jonathan Schooler, a Canadian Researcher, an average mind wanders away from the task at hand from 15 - 20 percent of the time.

Knowing that you are not alone will not help you with the problem. For you to improve your focus, you need first to determine the root cause of your issue. If you have a challenge in focusing and this is your primary concern, then the following could be the root cause:

1. **Sleep Deprivation**

You should have already known that lack of enough sleep causes focusing issue. Remember that you are supposed to get at least 7 to 8 hours of sleep every night. This is surprisingly a hard requirement for most people due to their busy schedule. This makes them unable to pay attention to the tasks ahead of them. The solution to this is to give your sleep first priority and get a good night sleep as much as possible.

2. **Distractions**

This one is common especially now that we have so much gone around us at one particular time. Your challenge in focusing could be as a result of distractions around you. Some of the top distractions that most people have included; texting or talking on phone, social media, gaming and gossiping. These distractions are easy to get rid of by yourself.

3. **Stress**

Stress and focus are having some connections; this is according to the research by Dr. Jon Kabat-Zinn of MIT University. As we try to multitask and focus on several things at once, the stress level increases and the more we are stressed the harder it becomes for us to focus. You need to take some time to relax and get a mindfulness exercise.

4. **Lifestyle Factors**

The lifestyle you are living in can affect your focusing ability. Eating a balanced diet and balanced meals such as proteins, healthy fats, and complex carbs can boost your focus. Regularly exercising can also increase your productivity. Remember that you need to avoid things such as eating snacks and foods.

5. **ADHD**

If you find out that none of the above is affecting you, you probably have ADHD. Research shows that about 5 - 10% of children have ADHD or similar attention disorder. In addition to this, about 4 percent of adults have ADHD and less than 20% have been diagnosed or treated. You need to talk to your doctor if you are chronically restless, unfocused or disorganized.

By now you may have identified what is corrupting your focusing abilities. The good news is that each of these has a solution.

How to Overcome These Challenges

This is just a summary of the solutions to these problems that we have seen above. If you have chronic attention and focusing issue, that could probably be ADHD and to overcome this, you need to seek medical advice. For lifestyle factors, you need to change your lifestyle and adopt better practices such as minding your diet and exercising.

Relaxation and mindfulness exercise are effective ways to overcome stress. To overcome distractions, you need to find a better place to do your work. If for example, your phone is distracting you, you can switch it off and concentrate on the task at hand. You can use apps and software that blocks some sites that might be causing distractions when using the internet. Schedule your sleeping time to overcome the sleep deprivation challenges.

5 Surprising Challenges in Focusing That Even Professionals & Athletes Face

Right now, short attention span is very common in most people, and it is among the top health crisis that is expected to grow. There are those challenges in focusing that people struggle with making it difficult for them to focus on the task at hand. The sometimes can be seen as complications of short attention spans. The following are 5 surprising challenges in focusing that even professionals and athletes struggle with.

1. **Impulsivity**

This involves acting in a manner that you do not have aforethought of what you are about to do or say and not considering the consequences of the same. Impulsive people talk tactlessly, disrespectfully or say things without thinking. As a result of the inability to focus because your mouth is first engaged before the brain. For those who are focused, the brain is engaged first before actions.

2. Restlessness

This is also another challenge that people struggle with. If you are disruptive, restless and shows habits of constant movements like fidgeting, leg shaking, etc, all this is a sign of lack of focus.

3. Forgetfulness

Hardships and struggles in most people's life and career can contribute to forgetfulness. Some of the common cases include forgetting your laptop at work, forgetting where you place your keys and many more.

4. Shifting Attention

Most people even athletes and professional have trouble moving their attention from one thing to the other. This makes them unable to keep track of what is happening at the moment. People with this challenge also find it difficult to keep up with a conversation with friends.

5. Procrastination

This is also something that is significantly contributed by lack of focus. Many people wait until the last minute to complete the task they have pending. Rushing the last minute makes work to be done in a hurry and hence it is done poorly.

The above are common focusing challenges that people struggle with from now and then. This will help you to know where you are and understand where to start.

6 Little Known Foods That Will Make You Lose Your Focus

The brain is the most critical organ in your body. It is therefore important to keep your brain in its optimum condition for better focus and concentration. Do you know that some diets have a great negative effect on the brain, impacting your focus and memory? The following is a list of these 6 diets that will make you lose your focus.

1. Refined Carbs

These include sugars and highly processed grains such as white flour. They have a high GI (glycemic index) meaning that they are processed fast by our body and this creates high blood sugar and insulin levels. Foods with high GI have been seen to impair memory in both adults and children and this, in turn, will affect your focusing ability. Replacing refined carbs with whole grain or complex carbs is important.

2. High Trans Fats Foods

These are types of unsaturated fats meaning that they are industrial products. They are also known as hydrogenated vegetable oils. These fats are often found in margarine, snacks foods, frosting, and prepackaged cookies and in ready-made cakes. High intake of these fats lowers brain volume, causes poor memory, and increases Alzheimer's disease risk and cognitive decline which in turn cause you to lose focus.

3. Processed Foods

Food such as chips, instant noodles, sweets, ready-made meals, microwave popcorns, and other highly processed foods tends to have high levels of added sugar, salts and fats. These foods have been found to affect the brain and contribute to a decrease in brain tissue which can cause poor memory and focusing ability. Avoid processed foods and replace them with whole foods and fresh fruits and vegetables.

4. Aspartame

This is an artificial sweetener that is found in many sugar-free products. It is often used by people who want to avoid using sugars. This has been liked with cognitive problems and increases the brain's vulnerability which can affect the concentration and focusing ability.

5. Fish With High Mercury

Mercury is a heavy metal which is a neurological poison. When ingested, mercury is mostly concentrated in the brain, kidneys, and liver. The effects of mercury include brain damage, disruption of the central nervous system and other parts of the body. With time, the brain is affected and you will not be able to concentrate better or focus on what you are doing.

6. Sugary Drinks

Drinks such as sports drinks, sodas, energy drinks, and processed fruit juices have a negative effect on your brain. It also increases the risk of type 2 diabetes and Alzheimer's disease. Research has also shown that foods high in sugar can cause memory impairment which in turn leas to loss of focus and concentration.

The above 6 foods should be avoided as much as possible. This is because regular intake of these foods can have a great negative effect on your brain which can make you lose your focusing ability.

Success Stories to Prove That You Too Can Overcome Focusing Challenges

For quite a while, I didn't know that my health habits were contributing to the poor focusing ability I began to experience. I struggled to keep it together and t his was hurting my career so badly. I used to dismiss information that eating unhealthy food ruins your focus because I never saw any connection between the two. I used to stay awake until the night watching movies and social media. I realized that something was not right because everything was becoming unbearable. It's not until I came across the guide about how to overcome the focusing challenges. I began maintaining good health habits such as getting enough sleep and eating right. Immediately, I began to see positive change and since then, I have not stopped.

~ Silvia, CA

If you could tell me that I cannot concentrate on my lecture classes when I had a phone with me, I could not listen to you. I believed that I was fine in multitasking and technology. I never imagined that I could go for an hour without my phone. This because worse and I begin to lose focus on simple things that I needed to do. I often found myself rushing the last minute and had a huge pile of errands that needed to be cleared. Even after learning that this was bad and hurting to my clear, I was not willing to give up on some things. It was not until when I almost got fired because of failing to fulfill my duties. I always gave excuses and my boss was fed up with those excuses. I started muting my phone during office hours and even leaving it at home sometimes. I was surprised by how much work I did the first week. That is when I realized that distractions are real since then I have managed to find a balance between works and avoid distractions.

~ Harvey M. U.K

Realizing that concentration and focus is the key to success has made me invest time and resources in making sure that I remain focused on tasks I need to do.

~ Simon C.

Chapter 2

37 Expert Techniques to Boost & Improve Your Focus and Concentration Within 3 Days

Do you know that it is possible to start improving your concentration and your focusing ability in 3 days? In this chapter, we are going to give you 37 experts' techniques and tips to help you start improving your focus as soon as possible. With improved focus, you will become more productive in your life and your career.

1. **Get Rid of All Distractions**

Identify and eliminate all distractions (e.g. mobile devices, snacks, unread novels) around that are causing you to lose focus. You need to get tough about dealing with your distractions.

2. **Change The Environment**

If you find out that the environment you are in is making you be unable to concentrate and focus, find start with small tasks that requires 30 seconds of attention span and move on to tasks that require longer attention span a new place and see it your focus will improve.

3. Start What You Can Finish

If you keep on failing to finish what you started, try starting smaller things which you can finish and this will improve your focus and inspire you to continue to newer heights.

4. Take A Deep Breath

When under pressure, relax and take a deep breath. To stay calm and centered, focus on your breathing. This will help you apply focus on the task at hand.

5. Batch Your Tasks

Consolidating your tasks will help you find efficiencies and help you to concentrate and focus. Batched and focused effort will create amazing results.

6. Focus on One Thing

Choosing one particular thing you want to accomplish and fully immerse yourself in it will ignite your passion and facilitate your focus.

7. Addictive Distractions

Addictive behaviors such as social media, browsing favorite sites etc. are addictive little interesting nuggets that compromise your focusing ability. Try to distance yourself from these addictive distractions.

8. Don't Dwell on the Past

Accept that the past is over no matter how many times you try revisiting, regretting or analyzing it. It will just hurt you more and ruin your focus.

9. Align Your Focus With Your Values

Getting clarity on your values and what you want will automatically reduce your internal conflict and help you concentrate on your priorities and reduce distractions.

10. Ask Yourself Questions

In case you find yourself focusing on the wrong things, you can ask yourself a new question. A sample question to reset your focus can be; "What do I want to achieve now?"

11. Store Your Ideas in One Place

Ideas in your head, reminders, distracting thoughts are all distractions that you need to dump somewhere. So find a place to write them down and focus on one thing at a time.

12. Tweak Your Physiology

Maybe you need some movement, better posture, sitting up straight, or a different position in order to focus. Find what makes you naturally focus.

13. Track Your Progress

It is proved that feeling some sense of progress is very critical because it helps you to stay engaged in what you are doing.

14. Choose To Do It

Take each task like a choice, a chance or a challenge and not as a chore because if you see it as a chore your mind will wander off to other things.

15. Delay Gratification

Having the ability to delay gratification will help you stay focused and help you make choices based on how something will help you in the future.

16. Create a Routine

For maximum productivity, you need to start a simple routine. This will help you optimize your work and maintain your focus.

17. Set The Day's Priorities

People who are focused and are effective tend to have their day's priorities clearly defined. Based on what you want to accomplish, determine how you are going to spend your time.

18. Do Less & Focus On Tasks With The Best Payoffs

You will find out that sometimes you just need to do away with so many tasks and focus on a few that will pay off the most.

19. Do What You Enjoy Focusing On

This can also be finding your passion. Never tie your happiness and success on the end goal but instead so what makes you enjoy the process and the journey.

20. Never Chase Every Interesting Idea

If you chase everything, you will not get any of them. Look at your top priorities and focus on those. The secret is to treat ideas like a flowing stream of possibilities.

21. Edit Later

When you edit along the way, you will be putting yourself into analysis paralysis. You should, therefore, do things quick and dirty, finish and then come back later and edit.

22. Yoga Concentration Exercise

Yoga exercise is a great contributor to your focusing ability. The magical powers of yoga will boost your mind's ability to focus.

23. Increase Your Attention Span

Train yourself to remain focused even in a distracting environment. Start with small a task that requires 30 seconds of attention span and moves on to tasks that require a longer attention span.

24. Find ways to refocus

Sometimes you can get off track and you can even get off the path. To avoid this, you need to catch yourself getting lost, stop what you are doing and think about what you were doing.

25. Find Best Time For Your Routine Tasks

Determine a fixed time to do your common routine tasks. People have their brightest and most active hours which should be used to focus on your best.

26. Strive to Finish Tasks

Most people are unable to finish what they started and this ruins their focus. Finishing what you start will make you remain focused.

27. Focus on Things You Can Control

Another mistake people make is to focus too much on things they are beyond their control. Just get clarity on things you can control and act on them.

28. Don't Give Yourself Excuse

Sometimes setting unrealistic goals contributes to making excuses once you realize that you can't make it. So set attainable goals to minimize chances of making excuses.

29. Define What You Want To Achieve

The simplest way to stay focused is to know what you want to achieve. Make your goals simple and precise; make them a single line statement.

30. Keep Your Energy High

Some tasks and projects need you to keep your energy high. To do this, you need to define time for things such as eating, working, sleeping and exercise.

31. Understand Your Limits

Everyone has limits and when it comes to focus, you need to pay attention to your limits. Know for how long you can stay focused and what activities can you stay focused on.

32. Learn To Say No

Know what you are capable of doing and learn to say no. This will help you finish on what you start and create a great focus momentum.

33. Limit Task Switching

Do you have so many things to accomplish, make sure that you limit switching between tasks to avoid losing focus?

34. Have Fun

In order to sustain your focus, you need to have fun in all what you do by seeing and focusing on the positive side of it. Adjust your approach to be more enjoyable.

35. Know Your Mindset

Master your expectations, attitudes, and beliefs by always being positive. It's about making your mind align with what you are doing and believing that you can do it.

36. Meditate

Mindfulness is very helpful in boosting your concentration. Find a comfortable spot, sit comfortably, clear your mind by breathing deep and observe your inner dialogue without engaging.

37. Reward Yourself

Every day, make sure that you rate your focus on a scale of 1 – 5 and strive to improve your score the next day and by doing this; you will begin to improve on your focus. To stay motivated, reward yourself for every progress that you make.

Understand the Effects of Poorly Organized Workspace on Your Productivity

Scientists have proven that clutter in your home or at your work affects your productivity in a negative way. Poorly organized work desk at your office or home kills your mood, resilience and your ability to work productively. These disorganizations can cause stress and provoke both mental and emotional distress. The reason behind this is that most of the time, you feel like you have little or no control over your workspace and your life in general.

Cluttered Environment Restricts Your Focus

When you have a cluttered desk, your brain is unable to process information effectively. The opposite is also true that when you are in an organized workplace, your brain processes information effectively allowing you to concentrate on the task at hand. Clutter competes for your attention and this is very exhausting.

As clutter increases at your workplace, your brain will continue to wear down and this will cause frustration. When you are frustrated, you cannot focus on your work and your productivity will definitely go down.

It is therefore important to clear away all the clutter at your workplace. Make sure that you find time between your day to clear your desk this can be during break time or lunch. Go through everything and determine ones that you need and those you do not need. Get rid of those you do not need. When your workplace is organized your mind will be able to focus on what matters and you will become more productive.

How Managing and Organizing Your Emails Boosts Your Focus

An email is a productivity tool but the sad thing is that it ends up being a distraction. Everyone reads every email that gets to their inbox.

Constantly checking and replying your email throughout the day will eat up your time and corrupt your focus. It is therefore important to devise means to manage and organize your emails in order to boost your focus.

To manage your emails and remain the focus, you need to do the following:

1. Avoid Temptation To check emails

This is what makes people lose focus most of the time. The moment they get a notification about a new email they reach out to their phone immediately abandoning the task at hand. You can refrain from checking your email during your work hours. You can mute the notifications to stay undistracted.

2. Designate Time for Emails

We understand that emails can be very important especially if they are work-related. You should, therefore, set aside some minutes for email checking and replying. Some people avoid emails during their productive hour that is from morning hours to the afternoon. So you can set an hour after these hours to check your emails. This will help you stay focused during your active hours.

3. Find a Personal Assistant

A personal assistant will help you check your emails and reply to most of them. This will save you a whole bunch of time and help you stay focused on what matters. With an assistant, they will inform you in case they find an email that needs your personal attention.

4. Find Other Means Of Communication

Email is not the only way you can communicate with people. There are so many ways you can communicate. If it is a conversation, using an email, you will have a long annoying thread that will disrupt you as you try to catch up. Stay focused, get another mean of communication.

Ways to Boost Your Focus during Meetings

How many times have you found yourself wondering or daydreaming during a meeting? Most entrepreneurs and business people are always moving from one meeting to the other the whole day. This can lower their focusing ability and reduce their productivity. Being able to focus during meetings is critical and it is not only in meetings it can be in lecture classes, church sermon, and others. The following are practical tips to help boost your focus during meetings.

1. **Be Prepared Beforehand**

It is important to ensure that you are ready for the meeting beforehand. Some meetings can take long and therefore you need to have eaten something and had enough sleep. You can do a little exercise, have a yoga and meditation session and take a few deep breaths. This will prepare you psychologically and physically and therefore you will remain focused during the meeting.

2. **Take Notes**

This is an effective way to stay focused during a meeting. When you take notes your brain will be engaged at all times and you will not daydream. You don't have to write everything, write what is important such as action to take, an idea, the question to ask, or a point to make.

3. **Contribute to the Discussion**

Failing to contribute to the discussion is one of the main reasons why we tend to switch off. Being an active part of the meeting will boost our focus during meetings and even give your career a positive boost. Never be afraid to ask questions if you find something is not clear.

4. **Get a Re-Focus Strategy**

No matter how much you try to stay focused during a meeting, there are times your mind will wander away. You should be very mindful and when your mind starts to wonder, refocus. If you are looking at something else, look at the person who is talking and start paying attention.

With these strategies, you will be able to stay focused during a meeting and boost your productivity.

How to Optimize Your Concentration and Energy Levels throughout the Day

In order to make the most out of your day and achieve more, you need to optimize your energy level and stay focused through the day. Your ability to focus directly influences how well you manage your time. There are so many things that need your attention on one particular day and therefore you need to learn how to stay focused throughout the day. The followings are ways to optimize your concentration.

1. **Realize that Your Energy Fluctuates**

It is important to realize that both your physical and mental energy levels do not flow evenly throughout the day. During the start of the day, the energy is high but as the day goes by, you become worn out. To optimize your energy, assign your most difficult tasks to your active hours and leave the rest for later when your energy level will be low. This will lead to better focus and greater productivity.

2. **Choose The Right Location**

Your work environment determines your productivity and how focused you will be during the day. This does not necessarily mean that you should completely change your office; it can be as simple as reducing interruption at your workspace as we have seen in the previous section.

3. **Take Breaks**

Having short breaks during your work time will help you stay focused and restore your energy. Trying to work throughout the say will lead to fast burnout and stress. You will become less productive and compromise your focusing ability. Have regular breaks at least after 1-2 hours it can be a 5 minutes break.

4. **Create a 25 Minutes Focus Time**

If you are struggling with focusing, it can be wise to try having a focus period of about 25 minutes with 5 minutes break and repeat again. When you follow up on these smaller objectives, over time you will get better at staying focused.

Music That Gets You into Focus Quickly

Nowadays, it is becoming extremely difficult to stay focused. Social media, email, news and other busyness make it difficult for you to have full attention on a single task. However, you do not have to despair because there are things that you can do in order to stay focused. One such thing includes listening to music.

Experts revealed that music is capable of releasing dopamine which is a pleasure chemical that improves your mood. Music can help you increase your productivity and start your creativity. Not all music can help you in this; the following are 5 types of music that can get you into focus quickly.

1. **Nature Sound**

Nature sounds are effective in improving moods and cognitive skills. According to the study conducted by the Journal of the Acoustical Society of America, the natural sounds are very effective in boosting your focus as long as they are not distracting.

2. **Classical Music**

When focusing on a project, classical music from composers such as Mozart, Beethoven, Bach, and others can be helpful. Researchers from the University of Helsinki found out that classical music can alter gene functioning and these can lead to improved brain function.

3. **Music You Enjoy**

Personal preference is also very critical in the music's ability to boost your brain function. Research shows that when you listen to music you love, it allows you to increase your focus. This evokes positive feelings which lead to a great level of productivity and focus.

4. Customized Music

Researchers have customized instrumental music to aid in increasing focus and decreasing distractions. This neuroscientist has analyzed the brain functionality and regulated the emotion and memory allowing the listener to stay focused. Some characteristics are put into consideration in making customized music these include; recording style, intensity, musical key, and emotional value.

5. Music Without Lyrics

Some people may find music with lyrics distraction and therefore researchers experimented with music without lyrics. They found that participant has a positive improvement in their focus and productivity in their work environment.

CHAPTER 3

10-MINUTES DAILY EXPERT PRACTICAL TIPS YOU CAN IMPLEMENT TO IMPROVE YOUR FOCUS

Research reveals that nowadays, adults are not able to maintain their focus for more than 20 minutes at a time. This shows how serious people have lost concentration and this hurts their productivity. If you want to improve your focus, the following is a 10 -minutes daily practices that will help you rebuild and increase your attention span.

1. **Create & Use A Workday Structure**

In order to rebuild your focus and have control of your attention, you need to reconstruct your attention muscle. This can be done by subdividing your workday into manageable chunks and taking regular breaks in between them. Use 10 minutes in the morning to plan your day and subdivide your task against the time you have. Repeat this every day for better results.

2. **Create A Not-To-Do- List**

Unlike the to-do-list we are used to, it is advisable to create a not-to-do-list. Whenever you feel the urge to do something instructing such as social media, write that down as a not-to-list. This way, you will transfer that distracting though from your mind to a paper allowing you to stay focused on what you are doing.

3. Read long Books Slowly

Research from the Pew Research Center has shown that reading short content online has killed our ability to focus. It has taught our mind to look for quick answers instead of exploring complex concepts. For 10 minutes daily you can start breaking this trend by reading a long novel slowly.

4. Practice Concentration Exercise

Use 10 minutes daily to boost your focus by sitting still in a chair and practice the following concentration exercises. Focus on your breathing for five minutes; concentrate on opening and closing of your fist for five minutes. These exercises might seem crazy by they will challenge your focusing ability.

5. Have 10 Minutes of Mindfulness

Have a moment for you to meditate. Find somewhere quiet where you can have your 10 minutes of undisturbed mindfulness. Repeat this daily, and you will boost your focusing ability.

6. Have an Attentive Listening Session

Listening attentively is one way to boost your concentration. Take at least 10 minutes daily to listen to the other person talking to you during a conversation. Try not interrupting the other person and trying to recap on what they have said. Also, use connecting words such as Yes, Ok, I get it and others.

7. Have a 10-minute daily session for physical exercise

Working out is for both your body and mind. Researchers found that creating a 10 minutes session in your daily routine for exercising will increase your brain's ability to ignore the distraction and to stay focused.

Little Known Secrets That Leaders Use To Improve Their Focus

Do you ever find yourself admiring someone who seems to be very focused and productive? Do you often wonder what the secret behind their success in all these is? In this section, we are going to give you 5 little-known secret that successful people, including leaders, use to improve their focus.

Secret 1: They Realize That Focus is a Muscle

Bad habits that rob your attention are always dismissed as just bad habits, but they are little more than that. Think of it as a workout exercise to tone up your muscles whereby with constant and regular exercising, you will achieve those triceps, biceps or even 6 packs you have always dreamed of. The same case to these habits, with time they will be cemented in us. Successful people have already realized that and have replaced these habits with better ones and with constant practice; this too has also become cemented in them.

Secret 2: They Always Clear Their Head

No way can you focus when you have hundreds of things you need to do. Unresolved issues will just distract you. Learn how to clear things that do not help you out of your head as experts do.

Secret 3: They Set Ideal Location

Experts have realized that distractions hurt focus and productivity and therefore they ensure that they find a quiet location to work on their tasks. Create a distraction-free environment for yourself and see your productivity skyrocket.

Secret 4: They Have Learned Not To Be Reactive

Every time notification from Facebook, Twitter or WhatsApp pops up, we react to it immediately and abandon the task at hand. Experts and leaders have mastered the art of ignoring these notifications until they finish with what they were doing. Turn off that notification and preserve them for later.

Secret 5: They Get Enough Sleep

A recent study reveals that people who spend time on the internet surfing aimlessly is as a result of lack of enough sleep. Lack of enough sleep depletes your energy, self-control and focus and this harm your productivity in a great way.

How to Focus Despite Distractions around You

Do you find yourself reaching out to your phone from now and then to check what is happening on social media? Or find yourself reading emails one-by-one as they come? All these are bad practices that will rob you of your focus and productivity. Learning how to stay focused despite all the distractions around you is a very important thing and these are 5 ways to help you in that.

1. **Mute or Turn off Notifications**

People are tempted to think that this notification as not distracting because they last for 10 -20 seconds by research shows that the moment you are distracted it takes about 25 minutes to regain focus. It is therefore recommended that you should set time aside for emails before you get into your active hours. This is the best way to stay focused on a distraction environment.

2. **Establish and Stick To Your Daily Routine**

Creating a routine is one thing and sticking to it is another. A daily routine will help you improve your focus and concentration because you will do things automatically. This is one of the most effective productivity hacks that will help you in many ways.

3. Stop Multitasking

Multitasking ruins productivity and also causes people to make mistakes. When you focus on one thing at a time, you will be able to maintain your focus throughout the day despite distractions.

4. Prioritize Your Tasks

You might be having so many tasks to accomplish in one particular day. This can be overwhelming for you making you be distracted and lose focus and at the end of the day, you will have accomplished nothing. Luckily, there is a way around this, prioritizing your tasks based on the order of importance.

5. Have a Relaxation Time

With your busy schedule, you will need to have some time for yourself to regenerate. This is very important especially in ensuring that you maintain your focus. Most people tend to use social media as a way to relax but this is the worst distraction. Instead of this, take a walk or have a session of mindfulness.

The relationship between Negative Thoughts and Focus and How to Get Rid of Negativity

Negativity in life is so dangerous and can ruin your life and wear you down. Negative thoughts foster a lack of concentration and focusing. We spend most of our time in our mind worrying too much about the future, focusing on what leaves us dissatisfied and replaying our past. Unwanted and negative thoughts bar us from enjoying current moments distract us from dedicating maximum focus on what is important and drain our energy.

Negative thoughts tend to make us feel depressed and anxious but the good news is that it is possible to replace negative thinking with positive thinking. By doing this, you will notice a huge difference in your focusing, comfort, and happiness.

The following are 5 ways to get rid of negative thought and improve your concentration and focus.

1. Recognize Inaccurate Thoughts

Sometimes you will find out that our mind will convince us to focus on something that is not right or true. These inaccurate thoughts are the ones that foster negative thoughts. It is important to recognize these thoughts and challenge them with positive ones.

2. Challenge Negative Thoughts

Every time you recognize inaccurate thought, you should be swift to challenge it before it messes up with you. Try to apply logic to your thinking and think about other possible outcomes; this is an effective way to counter negative thoughts.

3. Practice Gratitude

Feeling grateful fosters happiness and positivity. Even if you are experiencing a difficult time in life, you should find little things to be grateful about. Keep a journal for yourself and write those things you are happy about, this way, you will get rid of negative thoughts and focus more.

4. Focus on Your Strengths

Human tends to focus too much on negativity and hence overlook the positive things in their life. It is important to practice on how to focus on positivity and your strengths. This way you will feel good about yourself and negative thoughts will not evade you.

5. Seek Help

If you struggle to manage negative thoughts by yourself, you should seek professional help. Sometimes negative thoughts can be too much in such a way that they prevent you from focusing and accomplishing your daily responsibility. So seek counseling and therapy sessions and this will help you.

How to Prevent Your Popular Gadgets from Reducing Your Attention Span

The abundance of technology in our lives is making it difficult for people to concentrate on long periods. Many people are finding themselves compulsively checking their phones and this compromise their attention in a great way.

Research has revealed that Smartphone compromises your ability to focus. This is one of the most common tech gadgets that are ruining people's ability to concentrate. Others include TVs, iPods, Video Games, and others.

The mobile phone has been noted to interfere with the cognitive performance of its users. Luckily, there are ways to prevent tech gadget from interfering with your focusing ability.

1. **Leave The Gadget At Home**

Most people might disagree with this but this is one of the most effective ways to prevent gadgets from ruining your attention span. Have days where you do not carry gadgets to your office. Instead, you can print out copies of the documents you need during the day. Start applying the techniques that were used even before the technology came to be.

2. **Limit You Data**

If it is completely necessary to use tech, you can limit its usage. The Internet is the most addictive of all and you cannot access the internet without data, so you can limit the amount of cellular data you use, and this will help you avoid distraction from your phone.

3. **Silence App**

Apps such as Facebook, email, Twitter, etc. are the most common when it comes to distracting people. You can silence these apps during your work hours or during the time you require maximum concentration.

4. Limit Your Screen Time

New iOS has screen time feature that allows users to limit the time they spend on certain apps. You can set this limit to a certain period of time. If you find yourself using your phone in bed, you can set this limit to help you avoid that.

5. Silence and Mute Notification

This can be the easiest way to ensure that your gadget does not eat up your productivity time. We tend to reach out to our phone every time we get a notification, and therefore we cannot concentrate on the task at hand. Muting notification and silencing your phone will help reduce distractions.

How to Permanently Get Rid Of Bad Habits That Deteriorate Your Focus

There are those habits that we engage in every day that rob us off out concentration and focus. The solution to this is to get rid of these habits. Most people struggle to change a habit, but the good news is that I will give you sure proof ways to get rid of habits that ruin your focus.

1. Stop Multitasking

This is one of the greatest habits that ruin your focusing ability. To solve this problem, be a completionist. Make sure that you finish what you start before taking on another task. Batching similar tasks is also another way to stop multitasking.

2. Get Rid of Distraction

Time wasters can be a bad habit that ruins your concentration. You should make it your mission to get rid of distractions in your life such as

TVs, Internet, Social Notification and others. In order to effectively get rid of these distractions, dedicate a special time to handle them.

3. Have a Plan

It's a bad habit to go by your workday without a plan. This will just make you waste trying to figure out where to start, what to do and what not to do. Create a work schedule and to-do-list and also prioritize on tasks.

4. Stop Being A Perfectionist

Perfectionism compromises productivity. It is, therefore, important to have changed this by setting your mind to focus on finishing and not perfecting. Be used to failure and accepting mistakes is something that can help you stop perfectionism.

5. Get Organized

Being disorganized is a great contributor to lack of concentration. Of your workspace is full of clutter, there is no way you will be able to concentrate. You should make it a habit to organize your place of work and make it neat to boost your focus and productivity.

Effective Exercise to Improve Productivity and Focus

Think of your mind as a muscle, and if you want to tone up your muscle, you need to exercise regularly. For you to attain maximum focusing ability and productivity, you need to start training your mind to stay focused on using the following exercises:

1. Memorization

Memorizing stuff is one of the effective ways of building and strengthening your mind muscles. Make it your goal to memorize something every week be it a poem or a verse of scripture.

2. Practice Mindfulness

Experts recommend that you should have about 10 -20 minutes of mindfulness meditation. You should also find time to practice mindfulness throughout the day. Know what you are doing, be in the moment and take one thing at a time. This way you will boost your focus.

3. Read Long Content Slowly

E-content is growing rapidly, and therefore people are now more attracted to content on the internet that content on books. It is good to read a book daily and read slowly. This is said to boost your focus, and if done regularly you will greatly improve your focusing ability.

4. Attentive Listening

This is yet another effective exercise to boost your focus and productivity. Listening keenly and trying to recall what has just been said is a great way to exceeding your focusing muscles. This is also an essential interpersonal skill that will make your conversation with friends to be an effective one.

5. Concentration Exercise

There are so many tools and gadget to help you in your concentration exercise. This will help you in boosting your focus. There are apps, games and online tools to help you in this exercise.

10 Affirmations to Strengthens Your Focusing Abilities

Our attention span is very low, and we need to do something to improve on this. The following are 10 affirmations that you can say to yourself at least 3 times a day in order to strengthen your focusing abilities.

1. I am free from distractions

2. I focus on one thing at a time

3. I have energy and clarity

4. I am highly organized

5. I am currently present in this moment

6. I am relaxed and focused

7. Right now I concentrate on this priority

8. I keep my goals and thoughts

9. Focus is commitment

10. My efforts in focusing are paying off.

Reciting these affirmations, from time to time will help you to be able to stay focused and stay productive.

Chapter 4

Summary of Key Action Plans

Congratulations for making it this far! You must have learned a lot in the previous sections. This section is meant to give you a recap, and a summary of key action plans to take in order to begin making changes to your life to achieve maximum focusing and concentration.

Understand Where You Are

The first step to attaining maximum focusing ability is first to understand where you are. You need to evaluate yourself and determine what affects your focusing ability. As we saw in the first sections, there are several causes of lack of concentration; these include distractions, ADHD, stress & depressions, sleep deprivation, lifestyle factors, and many others. These are the most common, and therefore you need to determine where you are so that you will know where to start.

It is also important to realize that when these causes of bad focusing ability get to another level, they can become a great struggle for you. These can turn to impulsivity, forgetfulness, shifting attention, procrastination, and restlessness. All these can contribute to poor productivity and short attention span.

Understand Your Lifestyle

Our lifestyle has really contributed to our low attention span. It is very distressing to find out that a joke about old fish having the shortest attention span is now on us. According to studies, the average attention span is about 8 seconds. This is very serious, and something needs to be done as soon as possible.

We have seen several ways to have a better lifestyle such as taking the right foods and exercising both your mind and body. The good news is that you are not alone in this, a lot of people; even professionals are still struggling with their short attention span. Furthermore, it is not impossible to change things; with persistence and consistency, you can change things.

Use Our 37 Experts Techniques

This is more of a handbook to that you can refer to anytime you need to remind yourself about something. Out list of 37 experts techniques will help you in improving your concentration and focus. These techniques are easy to follow and do not require so much from you. Within 3 days, you should start seeing results.

Conquer Distractions

You may have realized that distractions are the major cause of loss of focus and concentration for many people. It is therefore critical to ensure that you do your best to get rid of distractions. Tech distractions are also very bad and prominent nowadays. Refer to the guide on how to get rid of distractions and stay focused.

Make it a ritual

Using our 10-minutes daily practical, you can improve your focus within a very short period. You do not require dedicating a whole day to do achieve better focus, all that you need is 10 minutes. With consistent in this, you will start seeing positive results in a short while.

Give yourself positive affirmations, avoid bad habits, get rid of negative mentality and force yourself to be focused. In everything that you do every day, always practice mindfulness because as we have seen, we are living in a world full of distractions. It is impossible to get rid of all the distractions in this world, but there are ways you can be productive with these distractions around you.

Unleash your maximum productivity in everything that you do by boosting your focus and concentration using the techniques we have learned above. Never accept to move on in your career knowing well that you are doing nothing positive in it. This will wear out your energy, and it will not be enjoyable anymore to go to work every day.

Focus and concentration is the key to success. It doesn't matter whether it is in your career or business, being focused matters. You will find out that successful people always invest their time and resources to optimize their productivity. This is the reason why you will find out that they seem to accomplish a lot despite their busy schedule. You too can achieve the same results if you start taking actions now.

Refer to these actions plans to know where to get started. Take this book as a guide to help you achieve long-term concentration and focus.

Conclusion

It is clear that we are facing a serious problem with our attention and we need to do something about it. Luckily, there is a way out of every situation you might be facing. As we have seen in this book, there are solutions to the focusing problems you might be facing.

It has been noted that people learn a lot of information, but few take actions. This book is packed with an easy guide to boost your concentration, and if you take actions, you will succeed. The opposite is also true; if you do nothing, then nothing will happen.

Realize that a lack of focus and concentration have a negative impact on your productivity and success in things that you do. Make sure that you do something about it in order to have a better career and achieve happiness and success.

-- *Patrick Bradley*

www.ingramcontent.com/pod-product-compliance
Lightning Source LLC
Chambersburg PA
CBHW030736180526
45157CB00008BA/3200